SERIES

Living a
Holy Life

wesleyan
publishing
house

Indianapolis, Indiana

Published by Wesleyan Publishing House
Indianapolis, Indiana 46250
Printed in the United States of America

ISBN: 978-0-89827-369-4

Written by Wayne Schmidt.

Cover design by Kory Pence.

D-SERIES

A Life of Significance with Jesus

Everyone wants their life to count for something significant. People everywhere are spending their lives for fading artifacts and fleeting glory. Significance, value, legacy, and impact are the desired outcome of every investment. The desire of believers in Jesus Christ should be no different. Those who are true followers of Jesus Christ are to be interested in becoming more and more like Him. Following Jesus and getting closer to Him ***IS*** significance, value, legacy, and impact for a Christian.

The *D Series* works by connecting every person to a solid relationship with Jesus. The scope of what we can learn and live for Jesus is limitless. But this series will get every believer on the right path—no matter where your starting point is. Regardless if you are a new believer or a seasoned disciple, this series is filled with truth for every person in the local Church.

What is significant about the *D Series* is the expectation that participants will actually live what they are studying. It is not enough to fill our heads and hearts with Jesus. We must follow through and make sure His love and interest in others show up in our service and daily activity. In other words, Christlike, holy living results when we use our heads, hearts, hands, and habits to focus on and represent Jesus.

Give yourself, your time, and your focus to Jesus through the *D Series*. Live your beliefs out in Jesus everyday!

THE COMMUNITY OF SPIRITUAL FORMATION

To illustrate it simply, there are four areas to engage: the head, heart, hands, and habits. Start by seeking knowledge and understanding of Jesus Christ. This wisdom will enter your heart and miraculously transform it. A unified heart and mind leads to a wholehearted expression of love through compassionate service. This outpouring of compassion becomes a daily way of life where we are given daily grace by God's Holy Spirit to live a holy life.

Coming full circle—your growing wisdom, unified heart, compassionate service, and daily holy living—you are driven to a community of spiritual formation where every believer looks more and more like Jesus. The result is a solid relationship with Jesus and a lasting significance, value, legacy, and impact in the lives of those we serve.

Dr. Jim Dunn
General Director
Spiritual Formation Department
The Wesleyan Church

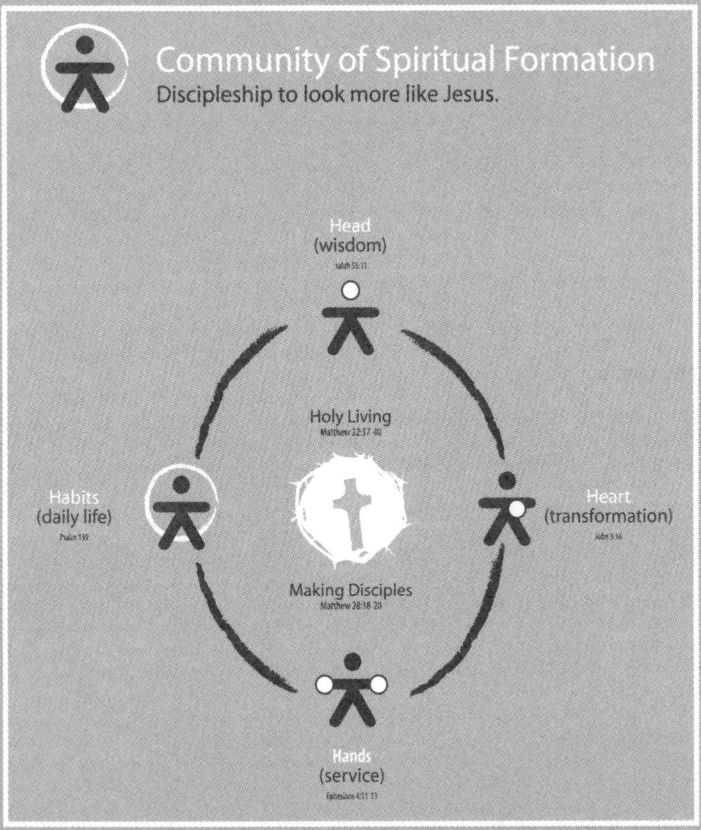

Contents

Introduction

From the time he was a boy he'd been drilled with the do's and don'ts of religious life. When he was young he excelled beyond his peers, earning the acclaim of his mentors. He rigorously played the religious game and actively opposed anyone who objected to its rules.

But as he aged, he tired and grew frustrated. In his own words, "For I have the desire to do what is good, but I cannot carry it out. For what I do is not the good I want to do; no, the evil I do not want to do—this is what I keep doing."

His search finally led him to the answer. He shared that answer with others. He wrote it down. For more than two thousand years, others have lived by his words. He is the apostle Paul.

Over the next several weeks you'll learn, in Paul's own words, how to get beyond the religious treadmill that leads to exhaustion and frustration. You'll learn about a relationship with Jesus, empowered by the Holy Spirit, that transforms your deepest desires and everyday behaviors.

Welcome to the adventure of living a holy life.

Transformation of Your Heart and Mind

COLOSSIANS 3:1-4

INTRODUCTION

May I have your attention, please? God wants our attention, and when we give it to Him, it leads to transformation. Our focus on Him is foundational to an empowered Christian life—today's passage describes it as a matter of life and death.

The life of Christ in believers changes us from the inside out through the power of the Holy Spirit. We then begin to see the world as God does.

Today you'll learn to focus your heart and mind so that you see the world as God does and make choices that give Him glory.

ICEBREAKER

When something is on your mind, how does it affect you?

Do you think much about heaven? What do you think it is like?

When someone says "it's a matter of life and death," what is the person trying to communicate?

DISCOVERING TRUTH—HEAD

When someone deeply desires something she may describe her intense feelings as "having my heart set on it." It's a way of communicating that this longing is of the highest priority and has become a focal point in her life. The apostle Paul is challenging us to set our hearts on something of ultimate importance.

On a blank sheet of paper draw something you once had your "heart set on." See if other members of the group can guess what it is!

> **When the Bible speaks of the heart it refers to the seat of all affections and desires. It is the epicenter of who we really are, buried deep beneath the layers of image, personality, attitude and behavior.**
>
> –Steve DeNeff, *Whatever Became of Holiness?*

Have a member of the group read aloud Colossians 3:1. What does it mean when Paul says we have been "raised with Christ"?

What does Paul encourage the Colossians to have their hearts set on?

Determined people may be described as "having their minds set" on a goal. One's mindset can make all the difference in whether they persevere or not. A team's mindset can be the difference between victory and defeat. In a similar way, Paul wants the Colossians to understand that a certain mindset is necessary to spiritual transformation.

Have a member of the group read aloud Colossians 3:2. What does Paul encourage believers to have their minds set upon?

> **It becomes us to spend this life only as a journey toward heaven . . . to which we should subordinate all other concerns of life.**
>
> —Jonathan Edwards, *Jonathan Edwards: Basic Writings*

The verse contrasts “things above” with “earthly things.” Have each member of the group suggest one example of each.

How do you take the focus off earthly things to develop more of an eternal perspective?

The Jewish people believed that God’s plan for salvation was to be hidden until the coming of the Messiah. At the coming of the Messiah, God’s peace and power would appear as promised by the Old Testament prophets. Paul may be drawing upon this belief from his Jewish upbringing about God’s salvation being “hidden” and then “appearing.”

Have a group member read aloud Colossians 3:3. What is hidden, and when is it hidden?

In what sense has a believer "died"?

Have a group member read aloud Colossians 3:4. What appears, and when does it appear?

Since a believer has "died" whose life is he or she living? What does it mean for Christ to be "your life"?

EMBRACING TRUTH—HEART

Draw a timeline of your life, with one end of the continuum being your birth and the other end today. Note on

If you read history, you will find that the Christians who did most for the present world were just those who thought most of the next. Aim at Heaven and you will get earth "thrown in": aim at earth, and you will get neither.

–C. S. Lewis, *Mere Christianity*

Christians should not shy away from the fact that our lives are centered on divine things. We offer a different way of making sense of reality and a different way of living.

–David Garland, *The NIV Application Commentary on Colossians/Philemon*

the timeline the periods in your life when your heart was really set on things above—you were very committed to seeking and honoring God. Then note the times when your heart was not set on things above.

Get into groups of two or three to discuss your timeline. Try to identify some of the reasons why at certain times your heart was set on things above. Also identify what may have contributed to those times when your heart was not set on things above.

When back together as a whole group, make a list along with other group members of common distractions that caused group members not to have their hearts set on things above. Share as well those reinforcements that helped group members have their hearts set on seeking God first.

When you see a person living with his heart and mind set on things above, what is it you see in him? How is that person's life different from the life of an unbeliever? How is that person's life different from a Christian who is distracted and preoccupied with earthly concerns?

What is one thing you might do to set your heart and mind more on things above? If you're willing, please share it with the group. Do you see some common trends in what has been shared?

CONNECTING—HANDS

Name three people who have encouraged you to focus more on Christ. What did they do to encourage you to have your heart and mind set on things above?

Name two or three people who right now might need your encouragement to focus more on things above. How might you encourage each to be more focused on Christ?

How does being around fully devoted (focused) followers of Christ cause you to focus more on Him? How does being around distracted (lukewarm) believers impact you?

On a scale of 1 to 10 (with 10 being most positive), how would you rate yourself in terms of your influence on others?

TAKE HOME—HABITS

Make a list of the "earthly things" that preoccupy you the most, either by causing you to worry about them or to be consumed by pursuing them. Once you have a list of three to five possible items, put a "1" next to the item that most preoccupies you. In a brief prayer submit that item, and your whole list, to God.

Think about your daily schedule. What are three little things you could do on a regular basis to center your heart and mind more on Christ—to exchange earthly things for an eternal perspective?

LOOKING FORWARD

Has there ever been an area in your life that you knew should be changed but you just couldn't seem to make the change? God has a plan to give us victory over these potentially powerful sins. We'll discover that plan next session.

DIG DEEPER

1. Read Mark 12:28–34. What does Jesus identify as the greatest commandment? Journal about some ways you can fulfill this greatest commandment in your life.

2. Read Romans 12:1–2. It seems God has a part to play and we have a part to play in renewing our minds. In a paragraph describe your part, and then add a paragraph to describe God's part.

3. Other passages in addition to Colossians 3:1 describe Christ as "seated at the right hand of God." Using a concordance or a Bible search tool such as www.gospelcom.net, examine places where this description occurs. Summarize what you have learned and share it with a friend.

OPTIONAL LEARNING ACTIVITY 1:

DISCOVERING TRUTH - HEAD

As a group, choose a devotional book that you will read together that helps you to set your heart and mind on things above. You may choose one of the classics such as *My Utmost for His Highest* by J. Oswald Sanders. Or you might choose a more recent devotional such as *Praying in the Wesleyan Spirit* by Paul Chilcote or *The Rhythm of Prayer* by Mark Moore. Each time you meet, have each group member share one insight from this devotional reading that challenged them to focus their attention more on "things above."

OPTIONAL LEARNING ACTIVITY 2:

EMBRACING TRUTH - HEART

As a group, schedule three hours for a "morning with God." Arrange to meet at your church or at a home that allows for group as well as individual time. If your group is so inclined, begin with a couple of Christ-centered worship songs or hymns. Then take turns reading aloud the book of Colossians together. After this reading, take an hour of individual time to journal about key insights from Colossians that prompt you toward a more Christ-centered life. Come back together as a group to share these insights. Then prayer around the circle to conclude your time together.

OPTIONAL LEARNING ACTIVITY 3:
CONNECTING - HANDS

As a group identify a couple of people you see as examples of individuals who have their hearts and minds set on things above. You may be drawn to this conclusion by the way they witness to others, by their calmness and confidence in the face of suffering, or by the way they live out their faith every day. Invite them to your group for an interview—be prepared to ask them questions that will help you to learn from them how to live a more Christ-focused life.

NOTES:

HEAD, HEART, HANDS & HABITS

The Conversion of Desire

COLOSSIANS 3:5–7

INTRODUCTION

God calls us to so much more than superficial conformity to a list of rules. God expects us to put to death sinful desires and live for Him from the inside out. Where God guides, He provides. He makes it possible for us to break the bonds of even the most persistent sins and fuels a desire to never return to those behaviors. Today you'll hear the command to embrace a deep-down change that brings a conversion of our desires.

ICEBREAKER

Share a brief sketch of your religious background. What were some of the religious rules (do's and don'ts) in your background?

Why do many Christians find it difficult to overcome sinful patterns?

Do most Christians think more about the "wrath of God" or the "grace of God"? Why?

DISCOVERING TRUTH—HEAD

Anyone who has planted a garden or cared for a landscape knows the ongoing challenge of removing the weeds. If you simply remove the part of the weed that's above the surface, it changes the appearance of the garden or landscape only briefly. The impact is cosmetic and temporary at best. It's when the weeds are pulled up by their roots that they are "put to death," which provides a more lasting solution.

Have someone in the group read aloud Colossians 3:1–7.

Notice the word *therefore* in verse 5. It's been said that when you see the word *therefore* in the Bible you should ask what it is "there for." Most of the time it serves to connect what has been said previously to what is being

> **Paul insists that the old nature is not renewed or reformed; instead, it is put to death. This forceful image means that Christian renewal is not some cosmetic overhaul of our sinful personalities. We do not simply add on a veneer of Christian values that only laminates our old nature and value system.**
>
> —David Garland, *The NIV Application Commentary on Colossians/Philemon*

said next. How do verses 1–4 provide the foundation for the command in verse 5?

What is it that believers are instructed to "put to death"? Of the items on the list in verse 5, which seem to be similar to one another and which seem to be different from the others?

Notice in verse 5 that "greed" and "idolatry" are described as being the same. How are they similar?

Select one of the items on the list and brainstorm as a group how you would advise a person struggling with it to "put to death" that sin.

> **The work of grace is inside out, so that private matters of the heart are always fleshed out in the public actions of the body.**
>
> —Robert Wall, *Colossians and Philemon*

Certain eras of church history have emphasized the "wrath of God," while others eras have placed emphasis on the "grace of God." While many people view the two as opposites, they are actually vitally related. "Wrath of God" is a phrase used throughout Scripture to signify His judgment on fallen creation. In His wrath God may remove the grace that we all need to put to death evil desires and live the holiest and best lives.

What does verse 6 indicate as a reason the wrath of God is coming?

Have someone in the group read aloud Romans 1:18–32. Notice that the phrase "God gave them over" is used repeatedly throughout the passage (see verses 24, 26, 28). What does that phrase mean?

God's wrath is shown in allowing people to act in self-destructive and sinful ways. Can you think of examples where people fulfilling their evil desires has led to their destruction?

One of the indications of a transformed life is things a person used to do are no longer done, and things they used to desire are no longer desired. These changes become part of the "before and after" story each believer has as a contrast develops between how you used to live and how you now live since Christ "is your life."

Read verse 7. Paul emphasized the same truth twice, once using the image of "walking" and then using the image of

The surprising thing about Paul's understanding of God's wrath is that the immorality and the foolishness is the punishment, not simply the cause for punishment.

–Ernst Kasemann, *Commentary on Romans*

Love slays what we have been that we may be what we were not.

–Augustine of Hippo

"living." What is the point Paul wants his readers to understand?

Paul's emphasis in verse 7 reinforces the command in verse 5 to "put to death" evil desires and the actions prompted by them. It's clear that Paul is not envisioning some cosmetic makeover where we simply manage to portray a different image. The challenge to get rid of sin goes to the deepest levels of who we are. What is the danger of believers taking the need for dramatic change too lightly?

EMBRACING TRUTH—HEART

Take a sheet of paper and draw a line down the middle. Label one side "before" and the other side "after." Seek to list three to five specific areas where you have seen God bring about a transformation of either your desires or your actions. If you're artistic, conclude the list with an image that captures your before-and-after story.

It can be helpful to review past situations in which God has given us spiritual victory over sinful desires in order that we might be prepared for future temptations. In the past, how have you "put to death" evil desires that belong to the earthly nature? Is there a pattern to this process—certain activities, attitudes, or steps that are crucial for a successful "crucifixion" of those areas that are contrary to a holy life?

The particular list of sins in verse 5 places an emphasis on sexual sins. In 1 Corinthians 6:12–20, Paul seems to indicate that there is something particularly devastating about sinful sexual desires and actions. After reading that passage, how would you describe the particular threat of sexual sin?

Undoubtedly Paul's list in verse 5 is uniquely tailored toward readers in Colosse who first received his letter, though it is relevant to all believers. Huddle in groups of two or three, and together create a list of the most perilous sins in society today. How is it similar to Paul's list? What are some differences?

CONNECTING—HANDS

How might the failure to "put to death" evil desires lead to the perversion of our relationships as brothers and sisters in Christ? In other words, how does sin not only affect the individual but have a relational impact as well? As a group, create a case study by describing a person caught in a particular sin. How would you warn or confront someone who claims allegiance to Christ but continues in sin?

Earlier you were encouraged to list some of the "before and after" differences you've experienced because of Christ. What would you say is the biggest change Christ has made in your life?

TAKE HOME—HABITS

Search your heart for any sinful desires or behaviors that need to be put to death. It may be helpful for you to read Psalm 51, where David is asking God to search his heart after being confronted by Nathan about his adultery with Bathsheba.

Is there an area of sin that seems very powerful in your life and keeps recurring? The ancients would refer to these as "besetting" sins. What might be the underlying desire at the root of this sin?

If you've identified sinful desires to "put to death," is there someone you can trust to pray with you and encourage you as you execute them?

LOOKING FORWARD

We were created by God with amazing potential. Sin has taken its toll on humanity, but God promises that we can be renewed through His power. We'll discover how to live a whole new life in the next session.

DIG DEEPER

1. Read Romans 6:8–18. As we put to death the power of sin in our lives, list what this passage would identify as "God's part" in the process. What does it identify as "our part" in the process?

2. Read Colossians 2:20–23. What do these verses describe as a completely ineffective means of putting to death our evil desires? What is the danger of changing our outward appearance but not experiencing the deep-down change Christ desires for us and makes possible?

3. Read Colossians 3:1–7. Journal about what you've learned so far from the verses covered in this study.

OPTIONAL LEARNING ACTIVITY 1:
DISCOVERING TRUTH - HEAD

Divide into two subgroups, men and women. Read again the list of evil desires that Paul enumerated in verse 5. As a group, create a list of what you would consider the "top five" threats of sin to your particular gender. Then identify a couple of strategies for each that would help a person of your gender avoid these sins or "put to death" the underlying desires.

OPTIONAL LEARNING ACTIVITY 2:
EMBRACING TRUTH - HEART

Write out your "before and after" story in less than one hundred words. It may help to think of your story in three movements: what my life was like before Christ, how I experienced Christ personally, and what my life has been like since Christ is living in me. Seek to include emotions or situations others could relate to. When your story is complete, share it with the group.

OPTIONAL LEARNING ACTIVITY 3:

CONNECTING - HANDS

Prayerfully identify people in your life, either Christians or non-Christians, who may benefit from hearing your story. Ask the group to pray with you and hold you accountable to seek an opportunity to share your story with at least two people you have identified.

Life Change—Personally and Relationally

COLOSSIANS 3:8–11

INTRODUCTION

The process of life change makes a deep-down difference in us, transforming our desires. As we've already learned and as our Scripture passage will emphasize today, that involves eliminating some attitudes and actions from our lives. True holiness, though, is far more than eliminating sin—it is experiencing a renewal that creates a whole new self. This renewal makes it possible for us to live a Christ-centered, Spirit-filled life. Today you'll discover the pathway to a whole new you.

ICEBREAKER

Many people struggle with change. Why?

How did life in the Garden of Eden for Adam and Eve differ from our lives in today's sinful world?

Why do some people have relationships only with those like them (economically, ethnically, and so forth), while others relate to a broad spectrum of people?

DISCOVERING TRUTH—HEAD

Our world seems to be filled with angry people. This anger spills over into all the environments of life—home, workplace, church. There's a real tendency to identify external causes for anger—a crazy driver, an incompetent coworker, an unruly child, or a frustrating situation. This results in people blaming others rather than taking responsibility for the tempest within them, short-circuiting their capacity to rid themselves of anger.

Have someone from your group read aloud Colossians 3:1–11.

Did you notice that verse 8 contains a second list of attitudes and actions that must be eliminated from the lives

> **What comes up in the bucket is usually what's down in the well.**
>
> –A Tennessee farmer, *The NIV Application Commentary on Colossians/Philemon*
>
> **Hunger and thirst are the strongest of all our bodily appetites. In like manner this hunger in the soul, this thirst after the image of God, is the strongest of all our spiritual appetites, when it is once awakened in the heart: Yea, it swallows up all the rest in that one great desire–to be renewed after the likeness of Him that created us.**
>
> –John Wesley, *"Upon the Sermon on the Mount"*

of believers? How does this list differ from the list in verse 5?

What does verse 8 command believers to do?

Do you think the five sins named in verse 8 are different types of sin, or all related to each other? Why?

There are many metaphors in Scripture that seek to describe the life change believers should prayerfully pursue. One of the most common is the picture of "taking off the old" and "putting on the new." The apostle Paul is using a metaphor

> **Prejudice hardens the arteries of the heart and cuts off mercy. It closes around us like a fist so that we can neither give mercy nor receive it.**
>
> –David Garland, *The NIV Application Commentary on Colossians/Philemon*

that draws from Jewish teaching where dress symbolizes a person's and community's relationship to God.

Have someone in your group read aloud again Colossians 3:9–10. Have another person read aloud Ephesians 4:20–25, which is another place Paul uses the old/new metaphor.

Divide your group into two subgroups. Have one subgroup list the attitudes and behaviors that Paul is commanding believers to "take off." Have the other subgroup create a list of descriptors used for what believers are to "put on." Then bring the subgroups together to share their findings with the whole group.

Colossians 3:10 describes the need for believers to be "renewed in knowledge in the image of [their] Creator."

This phrase reminds us of Genesis 1:26–27. Have someone from the group read it aloud. What is the value of believers knowing they are created in God's image? How would sin distort the knowledge of God's image?

We live in a world where people are divided by their differences—the rich rarely interact with the poor, and people of different ethnicities tend to stay within their own racial group unless forced to do otherwise. These prejudices impact people individually by hardening their hearts and impact people socially by stereotyping others who are different from themselves. But there is also a spiritual impact.

Colossians 3:11 describes differences between people that would have been present in the audience in Colosse. They might be characterized this way:

Racial and ethnic reconciliation will be a distinguishing mark, maybe even the distinguishing mark, of the next outpouring of God's Spirit.

—Brenda Salter McNeil, *The Heart of Racial Justice*

"Jew or Greek"—ethnic differences

"Circumcised or uncircumcised"—ethnic and religious differences

"Barbarian, Scythian"—cultural or class differences

"Slave or free"—economic differences

Taking these differences one at a time, how might each of them tend to cause division?

Colossians 3:11 ends by saying, "but Christ is all, and is in all." What do you think the word *all* refers to specifically? What point do you think Paul is making?

EMBRACING TRUTH—HEART

Verse 8 describes a variety of manifestations of anger. It's a reminder that the presence of anger shows itself differently in different people. What are some common ways that anger might be shown in people's lives? Are some more obvious and some more subtle?

Divide your group into four subgroups to identify ways unchecked anger can threaten the well-being of people and their relationships. Have a subgroup focus on the impact in each of the following:

Personally—health; emotional, mental, and spiritual well-being

Relationally at home—marriage, parenting, extended family

At work—relationships with coworkers, job performance

At church—relationships with other believers, capacity to serve and lead

Have the subgroups report back to the total group their conclusions, and if time permits, allow the whole group to brainstorm other consequences in each area.

How does a person "get rid of" anger? Create a roadmap with the steps that can provide freedom from anger. Then identify which steps are more "God's part" and which steps may be more "our part" in the process.

A Christian is commanded to "put on the new self." Using the analogy of clothing, the clothing is provided for us, but we have the responsibility to put it on. In what ways are Christians "new" because of Christ? Is it possible to be given a new self but not to put it on? What practical things can a person do to put on the new self?

Verse 11 lists differences that divided Christians in Colosse. Do some of these differences still divide believers today? Can you think of other differences that tend to divide Christ-followers and undermine unity?

CONNECTING—HANDS

So far in Colossians 3 we've covered two moral codes or lists of rules. Those listed in verse 5 have been characterized as "sexual" sins, while those in verse 8 have been called "speaking" sins. What are the "speaking sins" you are most prone to commit? List three strategies you can implement to ensure you honor God with your mouth.

Our unawareness of prejudice makes it powerful. Search your heart for stereotypes you tend to have toward certain types of people. Confess them in specific words to God, and ask Him to make you conscious of whenever they impact your relationship with another person.

TAKE HOME—HABITS

Media can undermine God's standards for our lives sexually or in our use of language. What change do you need to make in your media intake (TV, movies, Internet, and so forth) to help you "put on the new self"? Who can hold you accountable to make this change?

Create a list of people that you fellowship with on a regular basis. Are there any who are ethnically, culturally, or economically different from you? Identify at least one Christian who is different from you. How can you intentionally be in close fellowship with him or her?

LOOKING FORWARD

Do you see yourself as a chosen child of God, holy and dearly loved? We'll discover why *whose* we are makes such a difference in *who* we are in the next session.

DIG DEEPER

1. Read Ephesians 4:26–32. Can you identify perspectives into anger and speech in addition to the ones you studied in Colossians 3:8? What solutions to unchecked anger does this passage provide?

2. Read James 3:1–12. Journal about the insights this passage offers into taming the tongue.

3. Read Galatians 3:26–28. Compare it with Colossians 3:11. Both compare lists of differences that often divide people. What do you find on one list that you don't find on the other? What additional insight does Galatians give about the source of our unity that overrides our differences?

OPTIONAL LEARNING ACTIVITY 1:
DISCOVERING TRUTH - HEAD

Visit a Christian bookstore either in person or online to locate a book that gives a Christian perspective on anger. Have each group member purchase the book, or have one member of the group read it and provide an "executive summary." After reviewing the book, discuss as a group what you have learned. Have members share one insight they want most to incorporate into their lives.

OPTIONAL LEARNING ACTIVITY 2:
EMBRACING TRUTH - HEART

Do you live in a community that is racially diverse? If so, how might you connect more fully with people who are ethnically different from you? Perhaps you could schedule a time for your group to meet with a group from another church that is ethnically distinct from you. Or each of the individuals in your group could meet with an individual who is of a different race. Brainstorm a few questions you can discuss when meeting, such as,

How does our society tend to divide us by our race?

Are there certain prejudices you have identified in your thinking?

What are ways that we can show the unity we have in Christ?

After the meetings, debrief as a group about your experiences.

OPTIONAL LEARNING ACTIVITY 3: CONNECTING - HANDS

As a group, plan an experience to help you connect with people across economic or ethnic barriers. One possibility is serving an organization within your community that reaches out to the underprivileged. Another is to identify an individual who would benefit from the group's providing help or resources to them. Pray together before engaging in this service project, and debrief afterward about any key lessons from reaching across economic or ethnic divides.

NOTES:

HEAD, HEART, HANDS & HABITS

Motivated by Perfect Love

COLOSSIANS 3:12-17

INTRODUCTION

Our Western culture tends to be very individualistic, but the Bible continually reminds us that we are one family in Christ. Being filled with the Spirit of Christ should make a difference in our attitudes and actions toward others, including those who may be most difficult to love. The more the Spirit fills us, the more love flows from us. The identifying mark of disciples is our love for one another. Today you'll learn how Christ-centered, Spirit-filled living creates a whole new depth of relationships with others.

ICEBREAKER

How should the relationships of Christ-followers be different from those of non-Christians?

When you think of a person being described as "holy," who or what comes to mind?

Worship involves both teaching and singing. What does each contribute? Why are both important? Which do you relate to most naturally?

DISCOVERING TRUTH—HEAD

Over the centuries of Christianity there have been various attempts to describe what holiness looks like in a believer. These efforts have sought to link externals with the internal reality of being filled with God's Spirit. How people clothe themselves—what jewelry is allowed if any at all, the lengths of sleeves and hemlines, even the color of clothing to be worn—has often been used (rightly or wrongly) as an external measure of holiness. Today's passage helps you discover how you're to clothe yourself internally as a Christian, holy and dearly loved.

Have someone in your group read aloud Colossians 3:1–17.

Many waters cannot quench love; rivers cannot wash it away. —Song of Songs 8:7

Love makes everything lovely; hate concentrates on the one thing hated. —George MacDonald

The apostle Paul began verse 12 with three descriptive statements of believers. What are those three descriptions, and what might each statement communicate to his readers? How might the descriptive statements balance each other?

What are the five virtues mentioned in verse 12 with which believers are to clothe themselves? How would you define each of those character qualities?

In verse 13 Paul mentioned two additional virtues. What are they, and how are they different from one another? At the conclusion of the verse, what does Paul identify as the standard for our practice of these virtues?

One of the descriptions of the holy life is "perfect love." We are empowered by the Spirit to fulfill what Jesus identified

> **Holiness is first and always about love. Anything else is a rabbit trail. We will speak often of holiness as living with power, or as living without sin, or as a baptism of the Spirit, but in its purest form holiness is a matter of love.**
>
> —Steve DeNeff, *More Than Forgiveness*

as the greatest commands—to love the Lord with all your heart, soul, mind, and strength, and to love your neighbor as yourself (see Mark 12:30–31). Jesus clearly connected love for God with love for others, which Scripture repeatedly describes as inseparable. John Wesley called this "social holiness"—where God's divine grace transforms how we relate to others.

In verse 14, what virtue concludes Paul's description of the spiritually well-dressed Christian? What impact does this virtue have on all the others?

Is there any connection between the command to love in verse 14 and the reality that Christians are "dearly loved" in verse 12. How might the two be related?

The pursuit of peace has been the quest of humankind throughout all history. The presence or absence of peace has national, relational, and personal ramifications. It has become painfully obvious that lasting peace can't be humanly generated or sustained.

Have a member of the group reread verses 15–17 aloud.

This paragraph of Scripture repeatedly mentions Christ. List what each verse points out as a dimension of a life centered in Christ. What does each verse identify as our part in making that dimension a reality?

Verse 15 says that Christians are called to peace. What does it mean to be called to peace? Read Romans

The peace of Christ rules where the word of Christ dwells.
–David Garland, *The NIV Application Commentary on Colossians/Philemon*

A great many people are trying to make peace, but that has already been done. God has not left it for us to do; all we have to do is enter into it. –D. L. Moody

12:17–19. What additional insights do these verses give to a Christian's call to peace?

Verse 16 highlights the communication between believers. What different forms of communication are highlighted in these verses? If you have some dramatic or musical talent in your group, have one member choose a favorite psalm, another a favorite hymn, another a favorite worship song—then as the group bows their heads, have those three members read (or sing!) their selection.

In verse 17, what does it mean to do or say something "in the name of Christ"? Give some examples of what this might look like.

EMBRACING TRUTH—HEART

In verse 12 we noted three descriptors of who we are in Christ—chosen, holy, dearly loved. Rank the three, with "1" being the characteristic you find easiest to accept as true in your relationship with God and "3" being the hardest to accept. Why did you rank them the way you did? Why is it important by faith to accept these statements?

How might our feelings at times interfere with the reality described by these adjectives?

Note in verse 13 that at times we are to "bear with" each other (forbearance) and at other times we are to forgive each other (forgiveness). In other words, not every "relational rub" is an issue of forgiveness—sometimes we need to just accept others' idiosyncrasies. What is the danger of being so relationally fragile that every little difference between people becomes a forgiveness issue? On the other hand, what is the danger of dismissing something that really requires forgiveness and reconciliation? What is your natural tendency: to take things too personally or to dismiss them too easily?

Break into subgroups of two or three. Focus on the phrase in verse 13 "Forgive as the Lord forgave you." When wounded, how do we keep the focus on Christ rather than the one who hurt us? What steps would you recommend a person take to keep his or her focus on Christ? What Scripture might you recommend for the individual to read? Reassemble as a group and share your conclusions.

Let's get a little artistic! With a blank sheet of paper and some crayons or markers, draw three pictures of things that tend to "disturb the peace" for Christians. Verse 15 says we're to let the peace of Christ rule in our hearts—so try to picture those things about which we tend to commonly worry or get upset. Now the test—see if other group members can guess what you've drawn!

Verse 16 instructs us to let the word of Christ dwell in our hearts. What practices or spiritual disciplines help you internalize God's Word, move it from information in your head to transformation of your heart?

CONNECTING—HANDS

All of us have in our lives at least one E.G.R. (Extra Grace Required) person. These people give us the opportunity to put into practice the command "bear with each other." Name (not out loud!) one or more of these people in your life. What specific steps might you take to be more gracious toward them?

Is there anyone you need to ask for forgiveness? Is there anyone you need to forgive? Even if forgiveness does not lead to reconciliation with that person, it clears our conscience and frees us when we "forgive as Christ forgave us" (3:13). How can you strengthen your focus on Christ to develop a more forgiving tendency toward others?

To put verse 17 into practice, identify three people and what you'd like to say or do for each of them "in the name of Christ."

TAKE HOME—HABITS

Identify the area in your life or relationships where the peace of Christ needs to rule (3:15). Find a prayer partner and share that specific burden with that partner, asking that person to pray with you for thirty days about greater peace in that area.

In what way can you build the word of Christ into your life (3:16)? Identify a spiritual practice you can add to your personal devotional time or at a strategic point in your daily schedule to cause you to think and act more based on God's Word.

LOOKING FORWARD

In the next volume, we will look at becoming a member of a local church and how best to use the gifts God has given us to serve our brothers and sisters in Christ as well as those who haven't yet come to know Him. You will also discover what makes your gift to the body of Christ special.

DIG DEEPER

1. Read Matthew 18:21–35. From this parable of Jesus identify at least three realities about experiencing God's forgiveness in our lives.

2. 1 Corinthians 13 is the "love chapter" of Scripture. Read the chapter and list practical ways in which love is demonstrated. Put a "D" for difficult next to those on the list that you find most challenging, and "E" for easy next to those that require less effort. Then choose one you can focus on to improve your loving relationships with others.

3. To broaden your understanding of "all in the name of the Lord Jesus" use a concordance or Bible search tool such as www.gospelcom.net to locate other places where this concept is used. What are biblical examples of specific things we're to say or do in Jesus' name?

OPTIONAL LEARNING ACTIVITY 1:

DISCOVERING TRUTH - HEAD

Verse 12 uses the adjectives "chosen," "holy," and "dearly loved" to describe the way God values and sees His children. As an exercise of affirmation, take turns focusing on each member of the group, having other group members identify a God-honoring quality they see in that person's life. Continue this exercise until everyone in the group has had the opportunity to receive the insights and encouragement of other group members.

OPTIONAL LEARNING ACTIVITY 2:

EMBRACING TRUTH - HEART

If you as a group sense a need to grow in the arena of forgiving others, choose a book that you all can read that further describes biblical forgiveness. One such possibility is *Forgive and Forget* by Lewis Smedes (Simon and Schuster, 1984).

OPTIONAL LEARNING ACTIVITY 3:
CONNECTING - HANDS

As Christians we are to be "clothed with compassion." Plan an outing where your group can show compassion to those less fortunate.

OPTIONAL LEARNING ACTIVITY 4:
CONNECTING - HANDS

Some of the activities of worship described in verse 16 are practiced differently by different churches. As a group, visit a service at another church of a different ethnicity or liturgy. How did that church's teaching of God's Word and music differ from your own?

OPTIONAL LEARNING ACTIVITY 5:
CONNECTING - HANDS

The passage concludes by challenging us to "give thanks to God." Have each member of the group write a thank-you note to God and share it with the group.

NOTES:

HEAD, HEART, HANDS & HABITS